Animal Homes

A Bear's Den

Arthur Best

New York

Published in 2019 by Cavendish Square Publishing, LLC
243 5th Avenue, Suite 136, New York, NY 10016

Copyright © 2019 by Cavendish Square Publishing, LLC

First Edition

No part of this publication may be reproduced, stored in a retrieval system, or transmitted in any form or by any means—electronic, mechanical, photocopying, recording, or otherwise—without the prior permission of the copyright owner. Request for permission should be addressed to Permissions, Cavendish Square Publishing, 243 5th Avenue,
Suite 136, New York, NY 10016. Tel (877) 980-4450; fax (877) 980-4454.

Website: cavendishsq.com

This publication represents the opinions and views of the author based on his or her personal experience, knowledge, and research. The information in this book serves as a general guide only. The author and publisher have used their best efforts in preparing this book and disclaim liability rising directly or indirectly from the use and application of this book.

All websites were available and accurate when this book was sent to press.

Library of Congress Cataloging-in-Publication Data

Names: Best, B. J., 1976- author.
Title: A bear's den / Arthur Best.
Description: First edition. | New York : Cavendish Square, 2019. | Series: Animal homes | Audience: Grades K-2. | Includes index.
Identifiers: LCCN 2017048024 (print) | LCCN 2017049379 (ebook) | ISBN 9781502636461 (library bound) | ISBN 9781502636492 (paperback) | ISBN 9781502636485 (6 pack) | ISBN 9781502636478 (ebook)
Subjects: LCSH: Bears--Juvenile literature. | Animals--Habitations--Juvenile literature.
Classification: LCC QL737.C27 (ebook) | LCC QL737.C27 B4548 2019 (print) | DDC 599.78--dc23
LC record available at https://lccn.loc.gov/2017048024

Editorial Director: David McNamara
Copy Editor: Rebecca Rohan
Associate Art Director: Amy Greenan
Designer: Megan Mette
Production Coordinator: Karol Szymczuk
Photo Research: J8 Media

The photographs in this book are used by permission and through the courtesy of: Cover Bernhardt Reiner/Alamy Stock Photo; p. 5 Wildest Animal/Moment/Getty Images; p. 7 ArCaLu/Shutterstock.com; p. 9 Sharon Keating/Shutterstock.com; p. 11 Juniors Bildarchiv GmbH/Alamy Stock Photo; p. 13 Arterra/UIG/Getty Images; p. 15 Anna Kucherova/Alamy Stock Photo; p. 17 Richard Prudhomme/Alamy Stock Photo; p. 19 Ingo Arndt/Minden Pictures/Getty Images; p. 21 Linda Freshwaters Arndt/Science Source/Getty Images.

Printed in the United States of America

Contents

A Bear's Home **4**

New Words **22**

Index **23**

About the Author **24**

Bears are big.

Bears are strong.

5

Bears live in cold places.

They need to stay **warm**.

Bears make **dens**.

A den is a bear's home!

Dens are small.

Bears fit into them.

Bears can dig.

They make dens in hills.

13

Bears make dens under trees.

They make dens in trees.

15

Bears make dens under rocks.

They make dens in **caves**.

17

Bears make beds.

They use leaves.

They rest for the winter.

19

Bears get up in spring.

Cubs can be born.

They grow in the den.

The den keeps them safe!

New Words

caves (KAYVZ) Empty spaces in rock.

cubs (CUBS) Baby bears.

dens (DENZ) Homes of bears.

warm (WARM) Not quite hot.

Index

beds, 18

caves, 16

cubs, 20

dens, 8, 10, 12,
 14, 16, 20

hills, 12

rocks, 16

trees, 14

warm, 6

About the Author

Arthur Best lives in Wisconsin with his wife and son. He has written many other books for children. He has seen black bears in the wild.

About

Bookworms help independent readers gain reading confidence through high-frequency words, simple sentences, and strong picture/text support. Each book explores a concept that helps children relate what they read to the world they live in.